T0273223

God's C
Taking the
Declaration Seriously

To order call toll free 1-800-462-6420 or 1-717-794-3800. For all other inquiries please contact the AEI Press, 1150 Seventeenth Street, N.W., Washington, D.C. 20036 or call 1-800-862-5801.

ISBN 978-0-8447-7145-8
ISBN 0-8447-7145-7

The AEI Press
Publisher for the American Enterprise Institute
1150 17th Street, N.W., Washington, D.C. 20036

God's Country: Taking the Declaration Seriously

Michael Novak

The 1999
Francis Boyer Lecture

The AEI Press

Publisher for the American Enterprise Institute
WASHINGTON, D.C.
2000

Foreword

The essay printed here is the lecture delivered by Michael Novak at the annual dinner of the American Enterprise Institute for Public Policy Research in Washington, D.C., on February 25, 1999. At that dinner, Mr. Novak received AEI's Francis Boyer Award for 1999. The award was established in 1977 by SmithKline Beecham, in memory of its former chief executive officer, to recognize individuals who have made exceptional practical or scholarly contributions to government policy and social welfare. The complete roster of Boyer Award recipients is included in this volume.

The 1999 Boyer Award was presented to Michael Novak in recognition of his profound explorations of the ethical foundations of economic and political systems, which have secured his place as one of the most important thinkers of the late twentieth century. His groundbreaking book *The Spirit of Democratic Capitalism* has influenced such leaders as Pope John Paul II, Margaret Thatcher, Lech Walesa, and Václav Havel and was in wide underground circulation behind the Iron Curtain beginning in 1984. As a university professor, prolific author, journalist, and, since 1979, the

George Frederick Jewett Scholar in Religion, Philosophy, and Public Policy at the American Enterprise Institute, Mr. Novak has extended the boundaries of religious thinking into many areas of culture and politics—including capitalism and democracy, the American Constitution, ethnicity, sports, poverty, and economic growth.

Among Mr. Novak's many honors is the 1994 Templeton Prize for Progress in Religion. Created in 1972 by Sir John Marks Templeton, the prize serves as a counterpart to the annual honor accorded secular disciplines by the Nobel Prize. The Templeton Prize recognizes individuals who have shown extraordinary originality in advancing humankind's understanding of God and spirituality. Its recipients include Aleksandr Solzhenitsyn, Mother Teresa, and Lord Jakobovits.

The grandson of Slovak immigrants, Mr. Novak was born and raised in Johnstown, Pennsylvania. He graduated *summa cum laude* from Stonehill College in 1956 with a bachelor of arts in philosophy and English and *cum laude* from the Gregorian University in Rome in 1958 with a bachelor's degree in theology. He continued his studies at Catholic University and Harvard University, where he received a master of arts in 1966 in the history and philosophy of religion.

Mr. Novak has held professorships at the University of Notre Dame, Stanford University, SUNY Old Westbury, and Syracuse University. He worked in the presidential campaigns of Robert F. Kennedy, Eugene McCarthy, and Edmund Muskie, and in 1972 was the chief speechwriter for vice presidential candidate R. Sargent Shriver. During the administration of Ronald Reagan, he was U.S. ambassador to the Human Rights Commission to the United Nations and to the Helsinki talks in

Bern, Switzerland, and he served on the Board of International Broadcasting and as a member of the presidential task force of the Project for Economic Justice. In 1986 and 1987 he chaired the Working Seminar on Family and American Welfare Policy, which played a pivotal role in building the political consensus leading to the Welfare Reform Acts of 1986 and 1996.

Mr. Novak's numerous books include *The Open Church, Belief and Unbelief, The Experience of Nothingness, The Rise of the Unmeltable Ethnics, The Joy of Sports, Free Persons and the Common Good, The Catholic Ethic and the Spirit of Capitalism, Business as a Calling, The Fire of Invention*, and two novels. In 1998 he wrote, with his daughter Jana Novak, *Tell Me Why: A Father Answers His Daughter's Questions about God*. He has been a columnist for *National Review* and *Forbes*, was the cofounder of *Crisis*, and has published more than 500 essays and reviews in those journals and in *Commentary, Harper's*, the *Atlantic, First Things*, and the *New Republic*. An annotated bibliography of his major works to date appears in his essay collection *On Cultivating Liberty: Reflections on Moral Ecology* (ed. Brian C. Anderson; Rowman & Littlefield, 1999).

CHRISTOPHER DEMUTH
President
American Enterprise Institute
for Public Policy Research

Francis Boyer Award Recipients

1977	GERALD R. FORD
1978	ARTHUR F. BURNS
1979	PAUL JOHNSON
1980	WILLIAM J. BAROODY, SR.
1981	HENRY A. KISSINGER
1982	HANNA HOLBORN GRAY
1983	SIR ALAN WALTERS
1984	ROBERT H. BORK
1985	JEANE J. KIRKPATRICK
1986	DAVID PACKARD
1987	PAUL A. VOLCKER
1988	RONALD W. REAGAN
1989	ANTONIN SCALIA
1990	THOMAS SOWELL
1991	IRVING KRISTOL
1993	RICHARD B. CHENEY
1994	CARLOS SALINAS DE GORTARI
1995	GEORGE F. WILL
1996	ALAN GREENSPAN
1997	JAMES Q. WILSON
1999	MICHAEL NOVAK

The Francis Boyer Award is given annually by AEI's Council of Academic Advisers to individuals who have made exceptional practical or scholarly contributions to government policy and social welfare. It was established by SmithKline Beecham in memory of Francis Boyer, a former chief executive of SmithKline and a distinguished business leader for many years.

Introduction

Christopher DeMuth

I don't know what got into them, those hard-nosed business executives who sit on the American Enterprise Institute's Board of Trustees, back in 1978 when they invited a theologian from Syracuse University to move to Washington and join the Institute's research staff.

But they were onto something big, and no AEI appointment has been more prescient than that of Michael Novak to AEI's George Frederick Jewett Chair in Religion, Philosophy, and Public Policy, which was established through the generosity of the Jewett family, our former Board chairman Dick Madden, and the Potlatch Corporation.

Perhaps there was something in the air. In that same year, the Cardinal of Kraków, Karol Wojtyla, a profound anti-Communist who had fought religious and civil persecution first-hand, became Pope John Paul II. In two years, Ronald Reagan would bring to the leadership of the West a new, unflinching moral vocabulary that would shake Soviet totalitarianism to its foundations.

What was in the air was a new breath of freedom, which challenged the then-prevailing assumption that moral truth and political and economic necessity are separate, and often antithetical, domains—and insisted instead that they are one and indivisible. Michael Novak invigorated that air. At AEI, he wrote *The Spirit of Democratic Capitalism*, published in 1982; by 1984 it was in wide underground circulation behind the Iron Curtain. (The work was translated with Novak's clandestine permission and assistance—thus vindicating AEI's position on the importance of intellectual property rights in emerging markets.) All the revolutionary leaders of the 1980s attested to the influence of that book. In Poland, Solidarity itself appropriated the term "democratic capitalism" to describe the goal of its struggle against socialism; and in this decade, after the fall, Michael has been treated as a conquering intellectual hero throughout central and eastern Europe, including in his own ancestral Slovakia.

Soon he may be parading farther east. *Democratic Capitalism* has recently been published in Chinese in the People's Republic of China, and the Communist Party, by restricting circulation and excising the book's religious passages, can only heighten popular interest in its secrets.

At home, Novak's influence has been so pervasive as to become invisible, absorbed into the political and intellectual atmosphere, transforming the chemistry of discourse. When he received the 1994 Templeton Prize for Progress in Religion, I tried to explain to a group of student interns at AEI the achievements that had justified an honor bestowed on Mother Teresa, Billy Graham, and Aleksandr Solzhenitsyn. They were baffled and uncomprehending. Novak was like the Nobel Prize economist whose theories, radical and unsettling when first propounded, seem obvious to everyone who reads about them decades later in the *New York Times* news story. Today it is important to recall how bold it was in the age of Ralph Nader to use "capitalism" in other than a pejorative sense, and how outrageous it was to couple "capitalism" with "democracy" at a time when socialism, dressed up as "social democracy," still held the moral high ground. The subsidiary notions of "empowerment" and "mediating structures" were simply strange, although Novak would be the first to insist that the ideas they described were ancient.

Today these Novakian terms are commonplace, and the rhetorical shift registers tectonic shifts in practice and policy. The current popular prestige of private enterprise and entrepreneurship would never have come to pass if the market economy had continued to be understood as a value-free engine of material welfare and personal gratification, rather than as an intrinsically noble and morally exacting institution—what Novak calls "business as a calling." The exciting devolution of social welfare programs and schooling from government to church, community, and other private organizations would never have come so far in the name of budget cutting and fiscal rectitude. The decisive change has resulted from renewed appreciation of the advantages of voluntary, spontaneous social organization, where questions of conduct, ethics, and self-mastery are central to the business at hand.

Today the risks we face are very different ones: those of success and of forgetting the truths that brought us to where we are. We are told that there is a "third way" to democratic capitalism, as if capitalism were something that needs to be tamed by government rather than the other way around. "Empowerment" is in such promiscuous use that it may, and often does, describe something bestowed by a government program or a tax credit, and thus is it twisted to the opposite of its true meaning, in service to the continuing effort to establish a direct and unmediated dependency of the individual on the state. Most serious is the resurgence, in trendy nineties garb, of the conceit that our astounding material prosperity is a mechanical, technological phenomenon—the economy on Internet autopilot, divorced from, and inconvenienced by, issues of character and culture and our Western heritage of religious teachings and ethical precepts.

But Michael Novak does not believe in "compartmentalization." His great appeal (akin to that of John Paul II and Ronald Reagan) is the almost eerie serenity with which he appreciates and interprets modern aspirations without budging an inch from ancient truths. He has continued to write brilliantly on business ethics, social and economic policy, culture, and religion. In his latest book, *Tell Me Why*, coauthored with his daughter Jana, he has even taken on the one issue that dwarfs all others in delicacy and potential for social disruption—the religious instruction of one's own children.

It is immensely gratifying to everyone at AEI that this prophet who has been honored in so many countries should finally be honored at home. His Boyer Award is inscribed:

To Michael Novak

Theologian, philosopher, and moral ecologist—
Who has brilliantly cultivated
Gardens of religious and secular thought;
Who has instructed and inspirited
Democrats and capitalists
And other fighters for freedom and social justice.

The award consists of the first complete edition of the published works of St. Thomas More, a fifty-year project at

Yale University whose first volume appeared in 1963 and whose twenty-first, and last, in 1999. We have assembled the individual volumes in a custom-made bookcase designed after a cabinet Thomas Jefferson had constructed for his use at Monticello. For those of you who wonder why Thomas More should be embellished by Thomas Jefferson for this award, Novak will now tell you why.

God's Country:
Taking the Declaration Seriously

*I*n nine months, the church bells of Rome will begin pealing, clanging, tolling to open the third millennium since the birth of a Jewish infant born in poverty. Through him, knowledge of the Creator who knows and attends to individual nations and persons was spread to the Gentiles: a vision of a benign Governor of the universe, a gracious Providence, the undeceivable Judge of the consciences of all, the Source of Nature's Laws, the Guarantor through sacred oaths of the truthfulness of systems of justice. Through him, the Law of Moses became, as Blackstone put it, the font and spring of constitutional government.[1]

The "God Who gave us life," Jefferson wrote, "gave us liberty at the same time."[2] This God endowed every woman and every man with inalienable rights.

Five thousand years of belief in such a God, Alfred North Whitehead observed, made possible the rise of modern science.[3] The call to imitate the Creator imparted to discovery, invention, and creativity a profound and palpable joy. David Landes, in *The Wealth and Poverty of Nations*, says that the

Jewish-Christian "joy of discovery" was as responsible as any other factor for the economic breakthroughs of the West.[4]

And yet we come to the new millennium with a heavy question. Does the century about to begin mark our last? Is America a meteor that has blazed across the heavens and is now exhausted? Or, rather, is our present moral fog a transient time of trial, those hours cold and dark before the ramparts' new gleaming? Are we nearing our end, or at a new beginning?

Looking Back 100 Years

Just a century ago, in 1899, 50 million of the 75 million people of the United States lived in rural areas. Most had no plumbing or electricity, or any transport except the horse. Ordinary people endured cold, heat, darkness, stench, crowding, spoilage. But 80 percent of households were headed by a married couple, and the federal government spent about 2 percent of the gross national product.[5]

In the 100 years since 1899, the United States has been much tested—by the harsh and bitter shock of Argonne; by the lows of the Great Depression; by the agonies of Omaha Beach and the biting cold of the Korean peninsula and the steaming heat of Quang Ngai—and has endured wrenching and transforming change: from tail-fins, Ike, and Elvis to flower children and the march on the Pentagon; from Martin Luther King's letterwriting in a Birmingham jail to Colin Powell's becoming chairman of the Joint Chiefs of Staff; from McCarthyism to the collapse of the myth of socialist inevitability in the collapse of the Berlin Wall; from the Reagan tax cuts to the greatest extended prosperity in American history. Technologies we never heard of thirty years ago characterize our lives today: word processors, faxes, cell phones, e-mail, biogenetics.

Along this short road of 100 years, we have become powerful and rich. And what about our nation's soul? Five subterranean earthquakes have altered the ecology of souls:

- Our great Protestant establishment lost both its self-confidence and its religious convictions following World War II. The old Yankee elite of Boston, Philadelphia, and New York no longer sets the nation's moral tone.

- Remember the erudite and eloquent letters written by soldiers of the Civil War, educated in one-room schools and by the Bible? Then watch MTV. Our moral ethos has fallen into the hands of "popular culture."

- Throughout the last century, Europe looked up to America as a model for the world. In this century, our intellectual class has looked up to Europe as the model for America—social democracy, the welfare state, *Sweden*.

- Beginning in 1947, in the guise of becoming "neutral," our courts and law schools became hostile to religion in the public square.

- Confined by the courts to private quarters, religious people who act in public spaces are rebuked with ridicule and penalties in university employment and in the law.

Jolted by these five institutional upheavals, in a brief fifty years the great well of religious and moral self-awareness of the American public has been emptied of its living water.

Few today can understand the American proposition in the way our forebears understood it. Words central to the American creed, such as *truth* ("we hold these truths"), *liberty* ("conceived in liberty"), *law* ("liberty under law"), and *judge* ("appealing to the Supreme Judge of the World for the rectitude of our intentions") once formed a great and glorious mosaic across the apse of the republic. That mosaic has fallen to the dust, disassembled into tiny pieces. Fewer every year remember how it used to look.

The Present Crisis

As a disturbing consequence, nonreligious people are growing more hostile to the remaining Jewish and Christian impulses they detect in public life. Some portray religious people as outside "the American way," extremists whose aim is to impose "theocracy."

An opposite consequence is that serious religious people are becoming alienated from the American polity. This U.S.A. (they say) is not the partner with whom our forebears made a covenant. *This* is not an ethos we admire. We know and we admire Philadelphia, 1787, but that culture lives no more.

Other citizens want not to be judged by anyone. They abhor "judgmentalism." The ancient biblical maxim "Judge not, lest ye be judged" implied that God's standards are high. The modern maxim forbids standards altogether (they are harmful to self-esteem).

Thus has the ancient Jewish, Christian, and modern virtue of "tolerance" been undone. Tolerance used to mean that people of strong convictions would willingly bear the burden of putting up peacefully with people they regarded as plainly in error. Now it means that people of weak convictions facilely agree that others are also right, and anyway the truth of things doesn't make much difference, as long as everyone is "nice." I don't know whether "judgmentaphobic" is a word, but it ought to be. This republic crawls with judgmentaphobes. Where conscience used to raise an eyebrow at our slips and falls, sunny nonjudgmentalism winks and slaps us on the back.

In the absence of judgment, however, freedom cannot thrive. If nothing matters, freedom is pointless. If one choice is as good as another, choice is merely preference. A glandular reflex would do as well. Without standards, no one is free, but only a slave of impulses come from who knows where. That is sometimes dignified as the scientific view of man.

To the contrary, the whole point of liberty is this: every choice makes a difference, for the fate of every soul and for the fate of the republic.

Nature itself highlights liberty; it is unique to human beings. The God of Abraham, Isaac, and Jacob, says the Bible, values liberty so mightily that He created this vast expanding cosmos to show it off—so that somewhere in it, in at least one place, there would be creatures free to recognize their Creator's friendship, and freely to walk with Him.

The Creator called on humans to build a city on a hill (a "shining city on a hill," as Ronald Reagan taught us to amend it). This Creator called humans to learn from history how to build, eventually, a Republic of Liberty and Justice for all: a city, at last, worthy of such creatures as He had fashioned. They would have to do this by trial and error.

Fittingly, when the time was ripe, after the passage of thousands of years, in a city named for the Second Great

Commandment, "Thou shalt love thy neighbor as thyself"—Philadelphia—men proclaimed the independence of such a republic, invoking His just judgment and asking His protection. Will that protection last forever?

All history is proof of a law of moral entropy. Civilizations, given time, end badly. Surrounded in Washington by monuments that echo Greece and Rome, we are reminded daily of the fall of great republics and democracies. What hope have we that our nation will end differently?

There are lessons in this nation's covenant with God, of which the Declaration of Independence is the primary jewel.

The Covenant

During the first days of September 1774, from every region, members of the First Continental Congress were riding dustily toward Philadelphia, where they hoped to remind King George III of the rights due them as Englishmen. As these delegates were gathering, news arrived that Charlestown had been raked by cannonshot and that red-coated landing parties had surged through its streets.

The gathering delegates proposed a motion for public prayer, that all might gain in sobriety and wisdom. Mr. Jay of New York and Mr. Rutledge of South Carolina spoke against the motion, because Americans were so divided in religious sentiments—some Episcopalians, some Quakers, some Anabaptists, some Presbyterians, and some Congregationalists—that all could not join in the same act of worship. Sam Adams arose to say that he was no bigot and could hear a prayer from any gentleman of piety and virtue who was at the same time a friend to his country. Mr. Adams was a stranger in Philadelphia but had heard that a certain Reverend Duché had earned that character, and he moved that the same be asked to read prayers to Congress on the morrow. The motion carried.

Thus it happened that on September 7, 1774, the first official prayer before the Continental Congress was pronounced by a white-haired Episcopal clergyman dressed in his pontificals who read aloud from the Book of Common Prayer the 35th Psalm:

> Plead my cause, O Lord, with them that strive with me, fight against them that fight against me. Take hold of buckler and shield, and rise up for my help. . . . Say to my soul, "I am your salvation." Let those be ashamed and dishonored who seek my life; let those be turned back and humiliated who devise evil against me.

Before him knelt Washington, Henry, Randolph, Rutledge, Lee, and Jay, and by their side, heads bowed, the Puritan patriots, who could imagine at that moment their homes being bombarded and overrun. Over these bowed heads the Reverend Duché uttered what all testified was an eloquent prayer, "for America, for Congress, for the Province of Massachusetts Bay, and especially for the town of Boston." The emotion in the room was palpable, and John Adams wrote to Abigail that he "had never heard a better prayer, or one so well pronounced. I never saw a greater effect upon an audience. It seemed as if heaven had ordained that Psalm to be read on that morning. . . . It was enough to melt a heart of stone. I saw tears gush into the eyes of the old, grave pacific Quakers of Philadelphia. . . . I must beg you to read that Psalm."[6]

In that fashion, right at its beginning, this nation formed a covenant with God, which it repeated in the Declaration ("with a firm Reliance on the Protection of Divine Providence") and in many later acts of Congress regarding Days of Fasting (for repentance) or Thanksgiving.[7] Let me quote from the Day of Fasting, December 11, 1776:

> Resolved, That it be recommended to all the United States, as soon as possible, to appoint a day of solemn fasting and humiliation; to implore of Almighty God the forgiveness of the many sins prevailing among all ranks, and to beg the countenance and assistance of his Providence in the prosecution of the present just and necessary war.[8]

Years later, in *Federalist* 38, Publius marveled at the unanimity improbably achieved among fragmented delegates from free states and slave, from small states and large, from rich states and poor: "It is impossible for the man of pious reflection not to perceive in it a finger of the Almighty hand which has been so frequently and signally extended to our relief in the critical stages of the revolution." Three times *The Federalist* notes the blessings of Providence upon this country.[9]

That has been our covenant with God. God wills free peoples to build communities in cities that gleam upon the hills, cities of virtue, and probity, and honor. God knows we are only fallen human beings, clay, poor materials for so grand a task. No matter. He calls on us.

Among the nations, no people has embraced that covenant so gladly as Americans. Their brightest jewel was the Declaration.

Michael Novak

The Declaration

On July 2, 1776, the Continental Congress voted, and on July 4 proclaimed, the Declaration of Independence of the United States. In that document, Thomas Jefferson twice referred to God in biblical terms, and before assenting to it, the Congress added two more references.[10]

The fifty-six Signers were, mostly, Christians; they represented a mostly Christian people; and it was from Christian traditions that they had learned these names of God. But the names they chose were entirely of Jewish provenance. Of names specific to the Christian faith the Signers were (wisely) silent, since it lies not in the competence of government to adjudicate theological differences beyond those essential for the common good.

Recall the four names that these Americans gave to God: *Lawgiver* (as in "Laws of Nature and Nature's God"); *Creator* ("endowed by their Creator with certain inalienable rights"); *Judge* ("appealing to the Supreme Judge of the World for the Rectitude of our Intentions"); and *Providence* ("with a firm Reliance on the Protection of divine Providence").

One of the names for God (Lawgiver) could be considered Greek or Roman. But Richard Hooker showed that long tradition had put Lawgiver, too, in a biblical context.[11] The other three names (Creator, Judge, Providence) derive from Judaism and came to America via Protestant Christianity.

That is not all. Implicit throughout the Declaration are four biblical *paradigms*: ways of imagining reality. First, this world had a *beginning*, was not an eternal cycle. Second, it was *created*—was not an accident. Third, on the entire cosmos was bestowed an intelligent and gracious *purpose*, a *Providence*. Fourth, this purpose of creation was to place human *liberty* in a kind of holy light, as captured in the hymn "America":

> Our fathers' God! To Thee,
> Author of liberty,
> To Thee we sing.
> Long may our land be bright
> With *freedom's* holy light;
> Protect us by Thy might,
> Great God our king.[12]

These four conceptions are neither Greek nor Roman notions. They are biblical. They arose from Judaism. Jerusalem, not Athens, is their birthplace. They gave our forebears an almost eerie confidence.

The God of liberty is not, and cannot be, a remote watchmaker God. Examine closely the God of the Framers. Like the God of the Hebrew prophets, this God plays favorites and, as an artist, delights in singular contingencies and ironic serendipities. In the Battle of Long Island, fog prolonged the night, allowing Washington's entire army to escape a British trap. This God exercises liberty. He makes choices. He chooses "chosen" peoples and "almost chosen" peoples and loves every people with a love unique to it.

For the Seal of the United States the Framers chose a motto that derives from Virgil, the Roman poet, but applies better to divine Providence in the biblical sense: *Annuit Coeptis,* "God smiles [approvingly] on our beginnings." If this be deism, it is a biblical deism. The God of liberty, like Providence, must love contingency and chance, since only in a universe arrayed in probabilities (not pure necessities) can individual freedom thrive.[13]

My point is not that our Founders were, on the whole, religious men (much less that they were Jewish). My point, rather, is that our Founders understood the drama of liberty in a biblical way. It is a mistake to say that they were solely, even predominantly, shaped by the Enlightenment. Of the founders of the French Revolution, that might well be said—but *they* passed by another route.

The American Signers thought of liberty in a biblical way—the way men think who are sinners, and know what sinners do, and how we must be checked, and how sentinels to our ambitions must be set in place by the ambitions of every other. "If men were angels," Madison wrote, knowing full well that men are *not* angels, and that the only moral majority that exists is all of us sinners.[14]

The high standards to which God calls a nation composed of Jews and Christians convict us all of sin. That we all are sinners is the elementary finding of biblical religion. That is why any republic built to endure must divide all powers and, as sentries to the common good, set proclivity against proclivity, so that a Republic of sinners, by sinners, and for sinners shall not perish from this earth.

The Framers loved the simple motto: "In God we trust." Its operational meaning is: "For everyone else, checks and balances."

But What Is Liberty?

The Signers thought of liberty, then, not as something given but as something learned, and learned only in a *social way* by the weight of an *ethos*; by public vigilance over *habits* and *behaviors*; by education in the *virtues* that make liberty a practice; by books of *exemplars* and *practitioners*; by *heroes*. They honored "moral ecology," holding that culture is prior to, and more basic than, politics or economics. Since culture shapes the habits of the heart, and habits are the tuned engines of our liberty, a polity neglecting them is suicidal. So wrote Samuel Adams in 1775:

> For no People will tamely surrender their Liberties, nor can any be easily subdued, when Knowledge is diffused and Virtue is preserved. On the Contrary, when People are universally ignorant, and debauched in their Manners, they will sink under their own Weight without the Aid of foreign Invaders.[15]

The Signers, then, thought of liberty as an achievement needing to be earned each day anew. A free people every day takes up responsibilities, with reflection and deliberate choice. But *laws*, *teachings*, and *official acts* are needed to protect an ethos of virtue, to diminish toxins in the air, and to drive away pollutants.

Equally, the first page of *The Federalist* shows how pivotal one act of liberty may be.

> It seems to have been reserved to the people of this country, by their conduct and example, to decide the important question, whether societies of men are really capable or not of establishing good government from *reflection* and *choice*, or whether they are forever destined to depend for their political constitutions on *accident* and *force*.[16]

Reflection and *choice* are themes the Bible taught our Founders. Through their families, they had many years' experience in testing *those* ideas in their own lives. Neither they nor their teachers believed that the lessons of the

Bible—or, for that matter, any moral teachings of the past—should lie about unused. Moral teachings should be subjected to experiment in the tests of daily living, *proved*, absorbed into one's flesh and blood. That is what the Founders meant by traditional virtues. Traditions live by new appropriations ("making one's own") in every generation; otherwise they die.

For the Americans, as Lord Acton saw, liberty is *not* doing what you wish or what you feel like. Liberty is doing what you ought to do.[17] Dogs and cats have no such choice; they do what instinct urges them to do. Humans are the only animals who have the choice whether or not to obey the higher law of their own being, whether to follow the better angels of their nature.

Here is the advice the author of the Declaration gave to Peter Carr, a young Virginian who wished to know how to live a life of liberty:

> Give up money, give up fame, give up science, give the earth itself and all it contains, rather than do an immoral act. And never suppose, that in any possible situation, or under any circumstances, it is best for you to do a dishonorable thing, however slightly so it may appear to you. Whenever you are to do a thing, though it can never be known but to yourself, ask yourself how you would act were all the world looking at you, and act accordingly. Encourage all your virtuous dispositions, and that exercise will make them habitual.[18]

What, then, is human liberty? After reflection and deliberation, to do what you are prepared to commit yourself to, in a way that others may count on. The capacity to practice that sort of liberty the Signers called "character." A man who acts from deliberation and choice they called a "manly" man. (*Manly* was not a term interchangeable with *male*.)[19] The woman who acts so they called a *valiant* woman. They believed that men and women need help from the surrounding society if enough of them are to act that way. They believed that, whatever may be said of a few of peculiar character, most people need the steel of religion if they are to be tolerably moral.[20]

As adherents to the biblical conception of freedom, the Signers were not sure that the American people of 1776 possessed sufficient virtue to bear the costs of war or, after it, the long, slow, grinding work of peace. John Adams expressed his nagging fear:

> I sometimes tremble to think that, altho We are engaged in the best Cause that ever employed the Human Heart, yet the Prospect of success is doubtful not for Want of Power or of Wisdom but of Virtue.[21]

Then, later, Abraham Lincoln warned in 1838 that the memories of the extraordinary virtues that the Revolutionary War taught were being leveled by "the silent artillery of time," as each generation became more remote from the originating spirit of the nation.[22]

What Is Virtue? What Is Character?

What did the Signers mean by virtue? They meant habits of self-control, calm reflection, sober consideration of costs and contingencies, courage, and that ability to persevere despite setbacks without which no difficult plan of action can be carried through to completion.[23] In other words, they knew the difference between people who pledge fidelity, chastity, courage, sacrifice, and, in general, reverence for moral truth, and then do not deliver, and those whose characteristic habits make their words more bankable than bars of gold.

Between a public fit for liberty and one fit for tyranny, good habits make the difference. The name for habits by which men act as slaves is vice.

The Signers held three principles: "*No republic without liberty, No liberty without virtue*, and *No virtue* [for most men, in the long run] *without religion*."[24] Of these three, we moderns have weakened on the last two.

These are the principles the Signers clung to when they dared to sign their earthshaking Declaration. Contemplating the many solemn oaths of loyalty they had sworn as subjects of the king; counting the costs of the impending war they were now accepting; weighing the consequences of a dreadful act of rebellion on which they would now embark, they pledged their lives, their fortunes, the safety of their families and their homes, and their good names as men who keep their oaths. All these they were prepared to lose, for liberty, if Providence did not permit them to prevail.

The Signers *taught* us what they meant by liberty by what they did and how they did it. Liberty sallies forth amid a troop of virtues, missing any one of which its resolve will surely fail. Benedict Arnold's commitment to liberty failed when one of his inner sentinels slept, perhaps the sentinel that checked his pride.

The Three Meanings of Self-Government

By this path, the Declaration gave the term "self-government" a triple sense. Obviously, the term means a massive shift in the form of government, from a monarchy to a republic. On a deeper level, self-government means a regime of self-mastery that requires higher virtues than a monarchy.[25] For self-government demands a degree of alertness, self-sacrifice, and responsibility that tests endurance. Obedience to law over time is onerous, and maintaining good habits when the good times roll is tedious. A prior generation may have risen to moral heights, and perhaps its sons and daughters will, in filial piety, maintain that level. But it is not in accord with human nature for later generations to keep that passion burning; it was not so, even in biblical times. "The silent artillery of time" thins out the ranks.

To refill the ranks, virtue must be summoned up. "A Republic can only be supported by pure religion or austere morals," John Adams wrote:

Public Virtue cannot exist in a Nation without private, and public Virtue is the only foundation of Republics. There must be a positive Passion for the public good, the public Interest, Honor, Power and Glory, established in the Minds of the People, or there can be no Republican Government, nor any real liberty: and this public passion must be superior to all private Passions.[26]

Why should this be so? Because liberty means acting from reflection and choice, yet often we find deliberation burdensome. Sometimes we *want* to act from passion before we have time to think. Sweet are the uses of perversity.

The third meaning of "self-government" is this: What in France they turn to *l'Etat* to do, and what in Sweden they turn to Social Democracy to do, in the United States people turn to each other to do, in their own undirected associations. "The first law of democracy," Tocqueville wrote, "is the principle of association."[27]

These are the three meanings of self-government embodied in the Declaration: a republican regime; a moral code of self-mastery; and a capacity for social organization independent of the state. All three enlarge and ennoble ordinary people, make them feel responsible, brave, and free, inspire them to do extraordinary things.

Is It a Declaration Merely of Self-Interest?

A final lesson of the Declaration is more profound. Most scholars give the Declaration a Lockean interpretation by which the fundamental human drive is a pre-moral principle—self-preservation. So powerful is the war of all against all that we surrender our capacity for violence to the State, and only then does civil society come into being.

Under the Lockean interpretation, each man has an interest in his own freedom, but feels no positive calling to end the slavery of others, except by an argument from an enlarged egotism: My safety is more assured in a larger community.[28]

But there is another interpretation—that of Abraham Lincoln. Under Lincoln's view, the need to end slavery is not egotistical but social. No man is an island. Each human is an integral part of one temple, one house. A house divided cannot stand. A house cannot remain half slave, half free (and I must add today, half pro-life, half pro-death). Either it will go all for slavery, or all for liberty. No man can properly will slavery (or abortion) for himself; hence, not for any other.

Madison, too, in arguing for religious tolerance, noted that creatures of God have duties to God *prior* to the formation of civil society.[29] There is a unity in us, as creatures of *One Creator*, that grounds in us a sense of what is due to others as others, of *what is right*, no matter how we feel about it.[30] This sense obliges us to defend the rights of others, not just our own.

In other words, as Lincoln said, "All honor to Jefferson— to the man who, in the concrete pressure of a struggle for national independence by a single people, had the coolness, forecast and capacity to introduce into a merely revolutionary document, *an abstract truth, applicable to all men and all times*, and so embalm it there, that today, and in all coming days, it shall be a rebuke and a stumbling block to the very harbingers of reappearing tyranny and oppression."[31]

The Declaration holds before us a vision, by which we have vowed to be measured. In the dead of night, as if foreseeing Lincoln's principle, Jefferson wrote: "I tremble for my country when I reflect that God is just."[32] This nation's covenant with the God of liberty cuts its shoulders raw with responsibilities.

The Apple of Gold in the Frame of Silver (Proverbs 25:11)

There is one more point to stress about our Founders: their lives, the success of their rebellion, all that they held dear depended on the strength and power of their *union*. If the apple of their eye was liberty, a golden apple, then the picture that framed it in silver was the Union.[33]

If the king divided them, they were finished. Among the friends of liberty, there was no room for discord between the South and the North, between the most religious and the least so. Everything was done to hold the Union firmly together. Union was the condition of every other good.

To that end, great efforts were made by leading religious preachers such as John Witherspoon,[34] the president of Princeton, and Samuel Cooper, who preached at Harvard for the inauguration of the Constitution of Massachusetts in 1781,[35] to show the consonance of faith and reason. Faith and reason, they held, are friends, not enemies. Our Founders stressed what faith and reason hold in common.

For instance: that it is hard to act with liberty, taking up full responsibility, without sometimes falling and needing to get up again and persevere. Such lessons they found in Plutarch and in Seneca, in Aristotle and in Cicero, as well as in the Book of Kings and Genesis and Deuteronomy. In Proverbs they found much that echoed maxims of the Greeks and Romans. From this, they drew much consolation. Their belief in a Creator of all things made it difficult for them to see a separation between the Creator and the laws the Creator placed in nature. They learned from nature willingly, as if it were another book of God.

The Union of all citizens, believers and unbelievers, is important in these months before the new millennium when, despite the surface calm, our country lies in grievous moral turmoil. Among Americans, some who are not religious, and some who are, speak as if the other were an alien race. For all of us, it is crucial to see that for America's fundamental principles we have *two* languages, one of reason, one biblical. For our Signers, actually, the language of the Bible *included* the language of reason; the language of reason gave practical force to biblical lessons. That is what Jefferson achieved in the Declaration. Its language is Jewish and biblical, but it is also the language of reason, or close enough to it for the generous mind to make translation easily.

This is the practical point I want to establish tonight. The Declaration ties us all together, nonreligious and religious. "United we stand, divided we fall." That was their motto then. It is still a sound motto.[36]

Our Founders did not intend this to be a nation in which Christianity was established as the federal religion. On the other hand, they did establish the principle that every state of the Union *must* have the constitutional form of a republic. And religion, they said often, is indispensable to the survival of republican principles. For instance, in George Washington's farewell testament: "Reason and experience both forbid us to expect that national morality can prevail in exclusion of religious principle."[37]

Our Founders learned—and taught—a *twofold* language: the language of reason *and* the language of biblical faith. They did not think that these two languages—at least as regards principles of liberty—were in contradiction. These two languages form a union. The Creator speaks both languages, and so can we. Thus spake the Declaration.

In our time, religious people have made the mistake of thinking that a culture war can be won by political methods. The two—culture and politics—are closely related in certain questions of law. But, mostly, they thrive in different spheres and must be addressed by different methods—even, usually, by different institutions.

Still, a peace between these two groups—the nonreligious and the religious—may demand more of the first than of the second. The nonreligious of today pursue a view that is far too narrow in holding that there is only *one* valid language, that of reason. In this way, they block their ears to half the music of this nation's founding. They fail to plumb the depths of Lincoln, Washington, or even Jefferson. In the name of tolerance, they themselves have failed to learn one of the two basic languages of many fellow citizens.

We need to repair the Union. We all have work to do.

Pessimism? Or Optimism?

Has the culture been lost? Is moral entropy unavoidable? Like Jefferson, we may tremble when we reflect that God is just.

Still, I heard a joke in Poland that I really like, on the difference between the optimist and the pessimist. The pessimist says that things are so bad they can't get any worse. The optimist says, "Oh yes, they can!"

A man I much admire, John Paul II, Karol Wojtyla, has a mordant sense of everything the other side can throw at us—the "culture of death," he calls it, not exactly a cheery prospect. But his favorite admonition is, "Be not afraid."

I heartily approve of his policy prescription too: *Think* with the pessimists. *Act* with the optimists. "With the pessimists" means without illusion. "With the optimists" means with a firm reliance on divine Providence.

Joseph Warren of Massachusetts stood with the Minutemen at Lexington and took a bullet through his hair above the ear. Two months later, just commissioned a major general in the Continental Army, he learned that 1,500 patriots had crept up Bunker Hill at night and silently erected earthen walls. Shocked at daylight to discover this, battalions of Redcoats were assembling for an afternoon attack. Some of them put all of Charlestown to the torch, and tongues of flame from 500 houses, businesses, and churches leapt into the sky. Breathless, Abigail Adams watched from a distant hillside and heard the cannons of the warships bombarding Bunker Hill for five long hours. As they did so, Joseph Warren rode to Boston and took a position in the ranks on Bunker Hill.

The American irregulars proved their discipline that day—and the accuracy of huntsmen firing in concentrated bursts. Twice they broke the forward march of 3,500 British troops, with fire so withering they blew away as many as 70 to 90 percent of the foremost companies of Redcoats, who lost that day more than a thousand dead. Then the ammunition of the Americans ran out.

While the bulk of the Continental Army retreated, the last units stayed in their trenches to hold off the British hand-to-hand. That is where Major General Joseph Warren was last seen fighting, as a close-range bullet felled him. The British officers had him decapitated and bore his head to General Gage.

Freedom is always the most precarious regime. Even a single generation can throw it all away. Every generation must decide.

Joseph Warren had told the men of Massachusetts:

Our country is in danger now, but not to be despaired of. On you depend the fortunes of America. You are to decide the important questions upon which rest the happiness and the liberty of millions not yet born. Act worthy of yourselves.[38]

Notes

1. "Upon these two foundations, the law of nature and the law of revelation, depend all human laws; that is to say, no human laws should be suffered to contradict these." *Commentaries on the Laws of England*, vol. 1 (Chicago: University of Chicago Press, 1979), p. 8. On the relation between revelation and natural law, see Blackstone's preceding paragraphs.

2. "A Summary View of the Rights of British America, 1774," quoted in *The Life and Selected Writings of Thomas Jefferson*, ed. Adrienne Koch and William Peden (New York: Modern Library, 1972), p. 11.

3. "When we compare this tone of thought in Europe with the attitude of other civilizations when left to themselves, there seems but one source for its origin. It must come from the medieval insistence on the rationality of God, conceived as with the personal energy of Jehovah and with the rationality of a Greek philosopher. Every detail was supervised and ordered; the search into nature could only result in the vindication of the faith in rationality. Remember that I am not talking of the explicit beliefs of a few individuals. What I mean is the impress on the European mind arising from the unquestioned faith of centuries." *Science and the Modern World* (Macmillan: New York, 1946), pp. 12–13.

4. See David Landes, *The Wealth and Poverty of Nations* (New York: Norton & Company, 1998), especially ch. 4,

p. 58, where he elaborates on the role of *joie de trou-
ver* in the economic development of the West.

5. Louis Hicks, research for a forthcoming AEI and Ben
    Wattenberg television project entitled "The First
    Measured Century." Another index of U.S. weakness:
    in 1891, eleven Italian immigrants, cane-workers in
    New Orleans, were brutally lynched. In protest, the
    government of Italy withdrew its ambassador.
    Nativists spread the rumor that Italy would dispatch
    five iron-hulled battleships to sail along the Eastern
    seaboard. The entire tonnage of the U.S. Navy did not
    equal that of even one Italian capital ship. The U.S.
    Navy lobby vowed that no such potential threat
    would ever arise again. That was the beginning of the
    U.S. "Blue Water Navy," which won the Spanish-
    American War a decade later. See Richard Gambino,
    *Vendetta: A True Story of the Worst Lynching in America,
    the Mass Murder of Italian-Americans in New Orleans in
    1891, the Vicious Motivations behind It, and the Tragic
    Repercussions That Linger to This Day* (New York:
    Doubleday, 1977).

6. John Adams to Abigail Adams, quoted in *America's God
    and Country*, ed. William J. Federer (Coppell, Tex.:
    FAME Publishing, 1994), p. 137. I have relied on the
    Federer account for this anecdote.

7. Consider passages from Acts of Congress in 1779, 1781,
    and 1782. The Congress thought it proper, for example,
    "humbly to approach the throne of Almighty God" to
    ask "that he would establish the independence of these

United States upon the basis of religion and virtue."
"Thanksgiving Day Proclamation of October 20, 1779,"
in *The Journals of the Continental Congress 1774–1789*, ed.
Worthington C. Ford, Gaillard Hunt, et al. (Washington,
D.C.: Government Printing Office, 1904–1937), 15:
1191–92. The following are longer extracts:

> Whereas, it hath pleased Almighty God, the father
> of mercies, remarkably to assist and support the
> United States of America in their important strug-
> gle for liberty, against the long continued efforts of
> a powerful nation: it is the duty of all ranks to
> observe and thankfully acknowledge the interposi-
> tions of his Providence in their behalf. Through the
> whole of the contest, from its first rise to this time,
> the influence of Divine Providence may be clearly
> perceived. . . . ["Thanksgiving Day Proclamation of
> October 26, 1781," ibid., 21:1074–76.]

It being the indispensable duty of all nations, not
only to offer up their supplications to Almighty
God, the giver of all good, for his gracious assistance in a time of distress, but also in a solemn and
public manner to give him praise for his goodness
in general, and especially for great and signal inter-
positions of his Providence in their behalf; therefore the United States in Congress assembled,
taking into their consideration the many instances
of divine goodness to these States, in the course of
the important conflict in which they have been so
long engaged . . . do hereby recommend it to the
inhabitants of these States in general, to observe,

and request the several States to interpose their authority in appointing and commanding the observation of Thursday, the twenty-eighth day of November next, as a day of solemn thanksgiving to God for all his mercies; and they do further recommend to all ranks and testify their gratitude of God for his goodness, by a cheerful obedience to his laws, and by protecting, each in his station, and by his influence, the practice of true and undefiled religion, which is the great foundation of public prosperity and national happiness. ["Thanksgiving Day Proclamation of October 11, 1782," ibid., 23:647.]

8. The preamble to this resolution reads:

Whereas, the war in which the United States is engaged with Great Britain, has not only been prolonged, but is likely to be carried to the greatest extremity; and whereas, it becomes all public bodies, as well as private persons, to reverence the Providence of God, and look up to him as the supreme disposer of all events, and the arbiter of the fate of nations. ["Fast Day Proclamation of December 11, 1776," ibid., 21:1074–76.]

9. *Federalist* Nos. 20, 38, 43. From France, Alexis de Tocqueville also took up this theme (*Democracy in America*, xi): "The gradual development of the principle of equality is a providential fact. It has all the chief characteristics of such a fact: it is universal, it is durable, it

constantly eludes all human interference, and all events as well as all men contribute to its progress."

10. Pauline Maier, *American Scripture: Making the Declaration of Independence* (New York: Knopf, 1997).

11. Richard Hooker (1553–1600) offers a taxonomy of the many meanings of *eternal law* and *natural law* in use for centuries: "I am not ignorant that by 'law eternal' the learned for the most part do understand the order, not which God hath eternally purposed himself in all his works to observe, but rather that which with himself he hath set down as expedient to be kept by all his creatures, according to the several conditions wherewith he hath endowed them. . . . Now that law which, as it is laid up in the bosom of God, they call *Eternal*, receiveth according unto the different kinds of things which are subject unto it different and sundry kinds of names. That part of it which ordereth natural agents we call usually *Nature's law*; that which Angels do clearly behold and without any swerving observe is a law *Celestial* and heavenly; the law of *Reason*, that which bindeth creatures reasonably in this world, and with which by reason that may most plainly perceive themselves bound; that which bindeth them, and is not known but by special revelation from God, *Divine* law; *Human* law, that which out of the law either of reason or of God men probably gathering to be expedient, they make it a law. All things therefore, which are as they ought to be, are conformed unto *this second law eternal*; and even those things which to this eternal law are not conformable are notwith-

standing in some sort ordered by *the first eternal law. . .* Wherefore to come to the law of nature; albeit thereby we sometimes mean that manner of working which God hath set for each created thing to keep; yet forasmuch as those things are termed most properly natural agents, which keep the law of their kind unwittingly, as the heavens and elements of the world, which can do no otherwise than they do; and forasmuch as we give unto intellectual natures the name of Voluntary agents, that so we may distinguish them from the other; expedient it will be, that we sever the law of nature observed by the one from that which the other is tied unto." Richard Hooker, *Ecclesiastical Polity* (Great Britain: Carcanet Press, 1990), book I, pp. 40–41.

12. Algernon Sidney, *Discourses Concerning Government*, ed. Thomas G. West (Indianapolis: Liberty Fund, 1996). See Thomas West's introduction, p. xxiii.

13. On the concept of emergent probability, see Michael Novak, *The Spirit of Democratic Capitalism* (Lanham, Md.: Madison Books, 1991), pp. 71–81; and Bernard Lonergan, *Insight: A Study of Human Understanding* (New York: Longman's, 1957), chap. VIII, sec. 5 and 6.

14. *Federalist* 51: "In framing a government which is to be administered by men over men, the great difficulty lies in this: you must first enable the government to control the governed; and in the next place oblige it to control itself. A dependence on the people is, no doubt, the primary control on the government; but experience has taught mankind the necessity of auxiliary precautions."

The Federalist Papers (New York: New American Library, 1961).

15. Samuel Adams to James Warren, November 4, 1775, in The Founders' Constitution, vol. 1, ed. Philip Kurland and Ralph Lerner (Chicago: University of Chicago Press: 1987), p. 668.

16. Federalist 1.

17. Lord Acton's famous formulation is "Liberty is not doing what one wishes; liberty is doing what one ought." Also, "Liberty and Morality: How they try to separate them, to found liberty on rights, on enjoyments, not on duties. Insist on their identity. Liberty is the condition which makes it easy for Conscience to govern. Liberty is government of Conscience. Reign of Conscience." "Liberty," in Essays in Religion, Politics, and Morality, vol. III, ed. J. Rufus Fears (Indianapolis: LibertyClassics, 1985), pp. 491–92.

18. Jefferson adds, a few lines later: "Nothing is so mistaken as the supposition, that a person is to extricate himself from a difficulty, by intrigue, by chicanery, by dissimulation, by trimming, by an untruth, by an injustice. This increases the difficulties ten fold; and those who pursue these methods, get themselves so involved at length, that they can turn no way but their infamy becomes more exposed. It is of great importance to set a resolution, not to be shaken, never to tell an untruth. There is no vice so mean, so pitiful, so contemptible; and he who permits himself to tell a lie once, finds it much easier to

do it a second and third time, till at length it becomes habitual; he tells lies without attending to it, and truths without the world's believing him. This falsehood of the tongue leads to that of the heart, and in time depraves all its good dispositions." See "Letter to Peter Carr, August 19, 1785," in *Thomas Jefferson: Writings* (New York: The Library of America, 1984), pp. 814–15.

19. See Harvey Mansfield's Bradley Lecture, "Is Manliness a Virtue?" October 14, 1997, available on *The American Enterprise* website: www.aei.org.

20. "Whatever may be conceded to the influence of refined education on minds of peculiar structure, reason and experience both forbid us to expect that national morality can prevail in exclusion of religious principle." George Washington, "Farewell Address," in *George Washington: A Collection*, ed. W. B. Allen (Indianapolis: LibertyClassics, 1988), pp. 521–22.

21. John Adams to Mercy Warren, April 16, 1776, in Kurland and Lerner, *The Founders' Constitution*, vol. I, p. 670.

22. "Address to the Young Men's Lyceum of Springfield, Illinois," in *Abraham Lincoln: Speeches and Writings 1832–1858*, ed. Don Fehrenbacher (New York: The Library of America, 1989), pp. 29–36.

23. On this part, see Christopher DeMuth's unpublished paper "Remarks at AEI Chairman's Dinner," December 10, 1998, and George F. Will, "The Primacy of Culture," *Newsweek*, January 18, 1999, p. 64.

24. Jeffrey Morrison, unpublished paper, "John Witherspoon on 'The Public Interest of Religion,'" prepared for presentation at the John Courtney Murray seminar, American Enterprise Institute, February 16, 1999, p. 18.

25. "For my own part I am so tasteless as to prefer a Republic, if We must erect an independent Government in America, which you know is utterly against my Inclination. But a Republic, altho it will infallibly beggar me and my Children, will produce Strength, Hardiness, Activity, Courage, Fortitude and Enterprise; the manly noble and Sublime Qualities in human Nature, in Abundance. A Monarchy would probably, somehow or other make me rich, but it would produce so much Taste and Politeness, so much Elegance in Dress, Furniture, Equipage, so much Musick and Dancing, so much Fencing and Skaiting, so much Cards and Backgammon; so much Horse Racing and Cockfighting, so many Balls and Assemblies, so many Plays and Concerts that the very Imagination of them makes me feel vain, light, frivolous and insignificant." John Adams to Mercy Warren, January 8, 1776, in Kurland and Lerner, *The Founders' Constitution*, vol. 1, p. 669.

26. Ibid.

27. Tocqueville, *Democracy in America*, vol. I, Henry Reeve text, as revised by Francis Bowen, ed. Phillips Bradley (New York: Vintage Books, 1945), p. 189.

28. "Jefferson's horizon, with its grounding in Locke, saw all commands to respect the rights of others as fundamen-

tally hypothetical imperatives: *if* you do not wish to be a slave, then refrain from being a master. Lincoln agreed, but he also said in substance: he who wills freedom for himself must simultaneously will freedom for others. . . . Because all men by nature have an equal right to justice, all men have an equal duty to do justice." Harry Jaffa, *The Crisis of the House Divided* (Chicago: University of Chicago Press, 1959), p. 326.

29. "It is the duty of every man to render to the Creator such homage, and such only, as he believes to be acceptable to him. This duty is precedent, both in order of time and degree of obligation, to the claims of civil society. Before any man can be considered as a member of civil society, he must be considered as a subject of the Governor of the universe." James Madison, "Memorial and Remonstrance against Religious Assessments," Amendment I, 43, in Kurland and Lerner, *The Founders' Constitution*, vol. I, p. 82.

30. "The concept of *what is right* is the concept of an objective condition, a condition discernible by reason. 'All I ask for the negro is that if you do not like him, let him alone,' said Lincoln, with a pathos which anticipates the war years. But his meaning is that the test of right is not how something agrees with our passions but how it agrees with a discernment of what is due to a man. Right conceived as subjective passion does *not* forbid us to do what is objectively wrong; it only directs us to do whatever we deem necessary for *our* lives and *our* liberty. Right conceived as a state or condition in which every man is rendered his due forbids us to dissociate

the value to ourselves of our own lives and liberties and the value to themselves of the lives and liberties of any men who may be affected by our actions." Jaffa, *The House Divided*, p. 329.

31. Letter to Henry L. Pierce and Others, April 6, 1859, in *Abraham Lincoln: Speeches and Writings, 1859–1865*, ed. Don Fehrenbacher (New York: The Library of America: 1989), p. 19.

32. To this famous sentence, Jefferson added: "I think a change already perceptible, since the origin of the present revolution. The spirit of the master is abating, that of the slave rising from the dust, his condition mollifying, the way I hope preparing, under the auspices of heaven, for a total emancipation, and that this is disposed, in the order of events, to be with the consent of the masters, rather than by their extirpation." "Notes on the State of Virginia," in *Thomas Jefferson: Writings*, ed. Merrill D. Peterson (New York: The Library of America, 1984), p. 289. These sentences indicate that Jefferson, too, saw the Declaration as an ideal already working in history.

33. "The assertion of that *principle*, at *that time*, was the word, *'fitly spoken,'* which has proved an 'apple of gold' to us. *The Union*, and the *Constitution*, are the picture of silver, subsequently framed around it." Abraham Lincoln, fragment, "The Constitution and the Union" (1860), in *Abraham Lincoln: His Speeches and Writings*, ed. Roy Basler (New York: World Publishing, 1946), p. 513.

34. "If your cause is just—you may look with confidence to the Lord and intreat [sic] him to plead it as his own. You are all my witnesses, that this is the first time of my introducing any political subject into the pulpit. At this season, however, it is not only lawful but necessary, and I willingly embrace the opportunity of declaring my opinion without any hesitation, that the cause in which America is now in arms is the cause of justice, of liberty, and of human nature. So far as we have hitherto proceeded, I am satisfied that the confederacy of the colonies has not been the effect of pride, resentment, or sedition, but of a deep and general conviction, that our civil and religious liberties, and consequently in a great measure the temporal and eternal happiness of us and our posterity, depended on the issue. The knowledge of God and his truths have from the beginning of the world been chiefly, if not entirely, confined to those parts of the earth, where some degree of liberty and political justice were to be seen. . . . There is not a single instance in history in which civil liberty was lost, and religious liberty preserved entire. If therefore we yield up our temporal property, we at the same time deliver the conscience into bondage." John Witherspoon, "The Dominion of Providence over the Passions of Men," quoted in Ellis Sandoz, *Political Sermons of the American Founding Era, 1730–1805* (Indianapolis: LibertyPress, 1991), pp. 529–59.

35. "We want not, indeed, a special revelation from heaven to teach us that men are born equal and free; that no man has a natural claim of dominion over his neighbors, nor one nation any such claim upon another. . . .

These are the plain dictates of that reason and common sense with which the common parent of men has informed the human bosom. It is, however, a satisfaction to observe such everlasting maxims of equity confirmed, and impressed upon the consciences of men, by the instructions, precepts, and examples given us in the sacred oracles." Samuel Cooper, "Sermon on the Day of the Commencement of the Constitution" (1780), ibid., pp. 627–57.

36. Between the religious and the nonreligious the relation is not symmetrical. For the nonreligious, it may be difficult to use religious language. For the religious, it is a quite familiar move to recur to the language of reason, a move often endorsed in the religious tradition. For the religious, one additional reason for trusting reason is that the Creator created it as well. Some of the nonreligious trust reason, but these days many don't.

37. Op. cit., p. 522. William Bennett collects several of these texts in *Our Sacred Honor* (New York: Simon and Schuster, 1997). Another source is James Hutson, *Religion and the Founding of the American Republic*, Conference at the Library of Congress, June 19, 1998 (Lanham, Md.: Rowman & Littlefield, 1999).

38. Quoted in Ronald Reagan's "First Inaugural Address," January 20, 1981, *Speaking My Mind: Selected Speeches* (New York: Simon & Schuster, 1989), p. 64. Regarding Joseph Warren's role at Bunker Hill, I have learned much from Catherine Drinker Bowen, *John Adams and the American Revolution* (Boston: Little, Brown & Company,

1950); David Ramsay, *The History of the American Revolution* (first published 1789), ed. Lester H. Cohen (Indianapolis: LibertyClassics, 1990); and Benson Bobrick, *Angel in the Whirlwind* (New York: Simon & Schuster, 1997).

www.ingramcontent.com/pod-product-compliance
Lightning Source LLC
Jackson TN
JSHW011943131224
75386JS00041B/1543

* 9 7 8 0 8 4 4 7 7 1 4 5 8 *